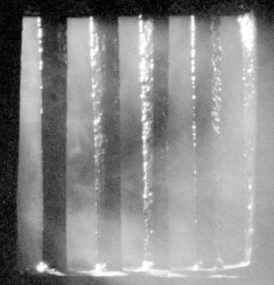

Here's to the wings of a Bird

(Inscription, Republican prisoner, August 1921)

© Government of Ireland 1995

Published by the Stationery Office

ISBN 0 7076 0479 6

To be purchased through any
bookseller, or directly from the
Government Publications Sales Office,
Sun Alliance House, Molesworth
Street, Dublin 2.

Written by Pat Cooke

Advisors: Professor Tom O'Neill
          Dr. Kevin Whelan

Designed by Creative Inputs

Separations by Master Photo Ltd.

Printed by W & G Baird Ltd.

Cover Illustrations
(Front Cover, from top left): Patrick Pearse; cartoon
of John Dillon in jail, 1888; Grace Gifford; mugshots
of Kilmainham Gaol prisoners, 1890s; Charles
Stewart Parnell; Robert Emmet; Eamon de Valera
celebrating victory in the East Clare by-election, 1917.

(Back cover): Detail, coiled serpents, from frieze over
entrance to Kilmainham Gaol.

OPW
Oifig na nOibreacha Poiblí
The Office of Public Works

A HISTORY OF KILMAINHAM GAOL 1796-1924

CONTENTS

Introduction

Uncommon Heroes

Kilmainham Gaol opened in 1796, four years before the Act of Union abolished the Irish Parliament in Dublin and replaced it with direct rule from Westminster. It closed in 1924, two years after the signing of a Treaty that restored a measure of independence to the twenty-six county Free State, a step that led ultimately to the declaration of a Republic in 1949.

Engraving of Kilmainham Gaol soon after it opened in 1796. Kilmainham Courthouse, still in use, is on the left.

Thus the opening and closing of the Gaol more or less coincided with the making and breaking of the Union between Great Britain and Ireland. During the intervening years the Gaol functioned like a political seismograph, recording most of the significant tremors in the often turbulent relations between the two countries. At the epicentre of these relations lay the Irish aspiration to political independence, setting off shockwaves of varying force throughout the nineteenth century and reaching a climax in the years 1916-22. There can be few places, therefore, that more intensely crystallize the forces that shaped modern Irish nationalism than Kilmainham Gaol.

A friend of the American philosopher and moralist Ralph Waldo Emerson once found himself imprisoned for reasons of conscience. When Emerson visited him he asked, 'Brother, why art thou here?' His friend replied, 'Brother, why art thou *not* here?' The exchange reminds us that under certain conditions the prisoner, ostensibly an outcast from society, can hold the high moral ground. This is a lesson deeply ingrained in the history of Irish nationalism, and one that helps us to understand the crucial role played by the County of Dublin Gaol at Kilmainham in Irish nationalist consciousness.

Nelson Mandela and Walter Sisulu secretly photographed in Robben Island Prison in the 1960s.

C: THE MAYIBUYE CENTRE

With the exception of only two of the really major figures, Daniel O'Connell and Michael Collins, it is possible to draw up a remarkably comprehensive list of Irish nationalist leaders who had been prisoners in Kilmainham in the years it operated as a prison. But while the fact that so many of them were associated with one prison is remarkable, their imprisonment in itself was not. The imprisonment of the leaders of freedom movements has been, and continues to be, critical in the history of many nations (Gandhi in India, Mandela in South Africa and Havel in Czechoslovakia are some notable examples). And just as men and women can be made into heroes through imprisonment, so can their places of confinement be exalted by their presence. In this way mere places of detention for criminals are transformed into powerful symbols of political freedom.

Why should this be so? Perhaps the key lies in the difficulty of finding convincingly positive and practical ways of defining Freedom, the aspiration that drives independence movements. Even on the lips of inspirational orators, descriptions of freedom can sound vague, tantalising, airy. But in its negative form - freedom defined through images of bondage, confinement, imprisonment - it can appeal powerfully to the popular imagination.

Honour in chains: A list of MPs and Parnellites imprisoned in Kilmainham and other gaols in 1881-2.

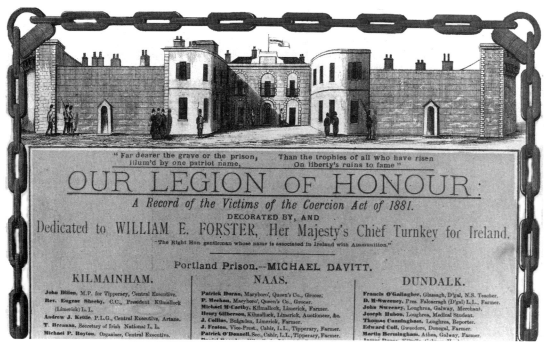

" Far dearer the grave or the prison,   Than the trophies of all who have risen
illum'd by one patriot name,   On liberty's ruins to fame "

OUR LEGION OF HONOUR:
A Record of the Victims of the Coercion Act of 1881.
DECORATED BY, AND
Dedicated to WILLIAM E. FORSTER, Her Majesty's Chief Turnkey for Ireland.
"The Right Hon. gentleman whose name is associated in Ireland with Ammunition."

Portland Prison.--MICHAEL DAVITT.

KILMAINHAM.	NAAS.	DUNDALK.
John Dillon, M.P. for Tipperary, Central Executive.	Patrick Doran, Maryboro', Queen's Co., Grocer.	Francis O'Gallagher, Glassagh, D'gal, N.S. Teacher.
Rev. Eugene Sheehy, C.C., President Kilmallock (Limerick) I. L.	P. Meehan, Maryboro', Queen's Co., Grocer.	D. M'Sweeney, Pres. Falcarragh (D'gal) L.L., Farmer.
Andrew J. Kettle, P.L.G., Central Executive, Artane.	Michael M'Carthy, Kilmallock, Limerick, Farmer.	John Sweeney, Loughrea, Galway, Merchant.
T. Brennan, Secretary of Irish National I. L.	Henry Gilbertson, Kilmallock, Limerick, Auctioneer, &c.	Joseph Hubon, Loughrea, Medical Student.
Michael P. Boyton, Organiser, Central Executive.	J. Collins, Bulgaden, Limerick, Farmer.	Thomas Cunningham, Loughrea, Reporter.
	J. Fenton, Vice-Prest., Cahir, I.L., Tipperary, Farmer.	Edward Coll, Gweedore, Donegal, Farmer.
	Patrick O'Donnell, Sec., Cahir, I.L., Tipperary, Farmer.	Martin Bermingham, Athea, Galway, Farmer.

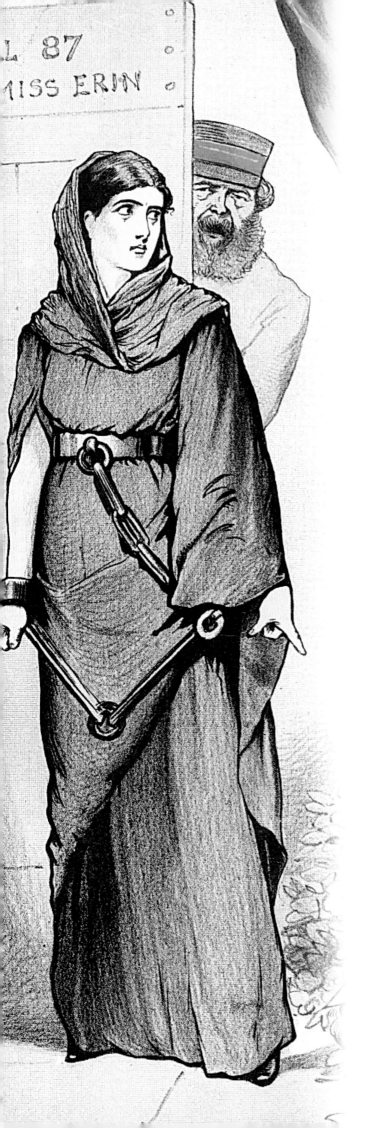

Some of the many images representing Ireland as a woman in bondage, a common motif in late nineteenth century nationalist imagery.

It is no surprise to find, therefore, that the Irish tradition of ballad and song abounds with tales of imprisoned heroes and images of bondage. To take one example, the song *A Nation Once Again* (at one time a virtual national anthem) speaks of 'ancient freedom' as something to be regained once the 'fetters' (ankle chains) of political bondage have been 'rent in twain'. The same is true of political imagery. The personification of Ireland as the oppressed maiden Kathleen Ní Houlihan became a powerful motif in Irish political cartoons and illustrations towards the end of the nineteenth century. She was frequently depicted abjectly confined behind bars or burdened with chains. This imagery made a deep impression on the generation of young idealists who led the 1916 Rising. The 1916

The captive imagination and dreams of freedom: The power of the prisoner image is forcefully represented in this 1888 cartoon of John Dillon, one of the Parliamentary Party leaders, in Dundalk Gaol. (Dillon was among the Parnellite prisoners in Kilmainham in 1881-2.)

Proclamation contains such an image; it declares the right of the people of Ireland to 'the unfettered control of Irish destinies'. By 1918 the electoral process had become devastatingly amenable to such imagery. In that year's general election the Irish Parliamentary Party, which had dominated Irish constitutional politics for over thirty years, was swept away by the radical nationalist party Sinn Féin. Many of Sinn Féin's candidates were then in prison. A famous election poster depicted the Sinn Féin candidate in convict dress and carried the slogan 'Put Him in to Get Him Out'. The connection between a prison record and electoral success could not have been more dramatically illustrated.

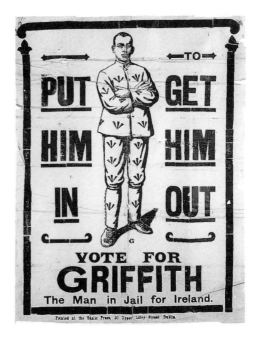

Political convictions: 1918 General Election poster.

Common Convicts

Kilmainham Gaol's historic importance was assured by those heroic men and women who were held or died here for their nationalist ideals. But there is much more to its history. After all, prisons are not built with the intention of turning people into heroes, but as places of confinement for common criminals. The Gaol's history as a prison, the fate of the common man and woman as convict, is a compelling story in its own right. Their story gives a unique insight into convict transportation and the Great Famine, two major events in the social history of modern Ireland.

Kilmainham Gaol is one of the biggest unoccupied gaols in Europe. Now empty of prisoners, it is filled with history. It has aptly been described as the 'Irish Bastille'. But unlike the Bastille, which became a symbol of the French Republic at the very moment of its destruction by a Paris mob in 1789, Kilmainham continued to mirror crucial events in the history of Ireland for almost 130 years, capturing in a unique way the history of a nation in the making.

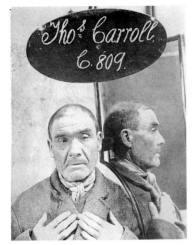

Mugshots of a Kilmainham prisoner, late nineteenth century. The mirror is used in the earlier version (left) to save using expensive photographic plates. In the later version, a split exposure captures full face and profile on the one plate.

PENAL HISTORY

Eighteenth century hopes:
The prison reform movement in Ireland, 1770-1800

Most eighteenth century gaols were places of cruelty, squalor and degradation. Many gaolers ruled over their charges with tyrannical powers. Often poorly paid, they saw prisoners as one of their main sources of income, and used ruthless means to extract a profit from them.

If the prisoner or his family were rich, he could have several rooms to form an apartment and all the drink and food he wanted. His family could even live in with him. But if he were unfortunate enough to be penniless or bankrupt, he could end up squatting on straw in a filthy cell on the brink of starvation.

A gaoler could be as arbitrary in his kindness as in his cruelty. At Naas, for example, the gaoler allowed the prisoners out for an hour each day to beg in the streets for their keep. Some gaols had a little grille in the boundary wall at footpath level where prisoners were allowed to beg from passers by. There were three such dungeon windows fronting onto Kilmainham Road at the Old Kilmainham Gaol. (The illustration above shows the begging grille at The Fleet prison, London, giving some impression of a similar arrangement at Kilmainham).

On the whole, gaolers, and by implication society generally, took little or no interest in the moral or spiritual welfare of prisoners. Prisons were about confinement, not reformation. Within the boundary walls of many gaols male, female and child offenders associated freely. Drunkenness and prostitution were common. When it came to imprisonment, the law made no distinction between children and adults. In prison, child offenders learnt the tricks of the thieving trade.

It was in a great wave of moral outrage against such conditions that the first efforts at prison reform began in the 1770s. The man who almost singlehandedly pioneered the reform movement was the English preacher John Howard (1727-1790). After visiting numerous prisons in Britain and Ireland, Howard wrote detailed reports exposing dreadful conditions. He began lobbying the British and Irish Parliaments for change.

His reforms concentrated on two main areas, separation and hygiene. Separation, the confinement of prisoners singly in cells, was necessary to break up criminal association and to prevent the spread of corruption, especially of young offenders by older ones. Hygiene was essential to stop the appalling prevalence of fevers. Gaol fevers killed far more than hangings, turning 'the penalties of the law into a lottery,' as Howard put it.

Howard's influence in Ireland was probably greater than in his native England, where the zeal for reform set in much earlier. Two Bills introduced in 1763 led to the setting up of a Prisons Inspectorate – sixteen years before England's Penitentiary Act – and the Prisoners' Health Act of 1778 led to the appointment of surgeons and apothecaries to visit prisons.

BY COURTESY THE EARL OF HARROWBY

John Howard Offering Relief to Prisoners, *by Francis Wheatley.*

In 1782 an Irish Parliamentary Committee reported on the *'Present State, Situation and Management of the Public Jails, Prisons and Bridewells of this Kingdom'*. Conditions in the existing gaol at Kilmainham came in for strong criticism. It was found to be:

> *extremely insecure, and in an unwholesome bad situation with narrow cells sunk underground, with no hospital. Through the windows of the prison the inmates conversed freely with acquaintances in the street from whom they procured instruments to assist escape. Spirits and all sorts of liquors were constantly served to the prisoners who were in a continual state of intoxication.*

In the course of a tour of Irish prisons in 1786-7, Howard visited the old Kilmainham Gaol and confirmed this poor impression. He found the inmates roaring drunk at eleven o'clock in the morning. The Gaol's windows faced the street, allowing 'a noggin or gill of that destructive liquor, whiskey' to be passed freely to the inmates.

Following this criticism, the Grand Jury of the County of Dublin decided in 1786 to build a new prison at the ominously named Gallows Hill. The site chosen (the present location) was consistent with Howard's recommendation that gaols should be built on elevated ground for ventilation, thereby helping to keep fevers at bay.

Construction proceeded rapidly. A report in the *Freeman's Journal* in July 1787 stated that the massive containing walls were already under construction. Howard himself inspected the site the same year. The stone used was limestone, which unfortunately has a tendency to weep in wet weather. The inmates of the new prison were to find the dampness having a deleterious effect on their health.

When the Gaol opened in 1796, it consisted of the gaoler's quarters at the front (the current facade, minus the protruding wings) and two rectangular cell blocks. The west wing in the present building was one of these blocks, while the East Wing was later demolished and replaced by the present spectacular structure.

Original plan of the Gaol. The original sections still surviving are highlighted. Numerous alterations were carried out over the years, the biggest being the replacement of the rectangular block on the right with the current East wing in the 1860s.

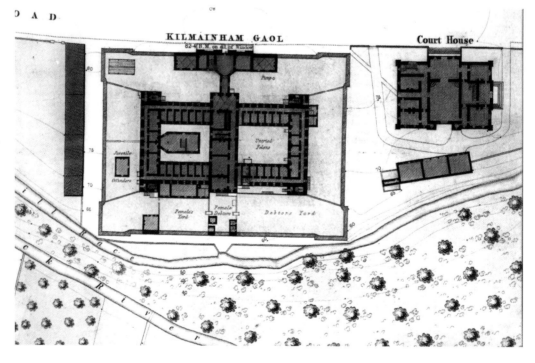

The most common crimes at the time the Gaol opened were assault, burglary, shop-lifting, pick-pocketing, rape, highway robbery, murder, bigamy, cattle-stealing, mail robbery, counterfeiting coins, and illicit distilling. But debt was by far the most common cause of imprisonment. Debtors comprised over half the prison population and took up almost half the Gaol's accommodation.

Nineteenth-century disappointments: poor conditions, transportation, the Great Famine

The great aim of the reformers was to replace the arbitrary aspects of the prisoner's fate with a just system of punishment. This could only be achieved however if the gaols were run according to professional principles of management. Unfortunately Kilmainham, having been built as a model of the new reform principles, soon disappointed the expectations of reformers in the way it was run. One of the depressing patterns of gaol history, from the time of the first reforms right through the nineteenth century, is the way in which the reformers' good intentions were constantly frustrated by the shoddy way prisons were managed.

The root problem from which so many other evils stemmed was overcrowding. Overcrowding made a mockery of the one prisoner to a cell principle, confirmed the reputation of prisons as schools for scandal, and led to poor hygiene and high levels of disease. Virtually from the day it opened, right up to the 1860s, overcrowding was to remain a problem at Kilmainham. Detailed evidence for this comes from the meticulous annual reports of the Inspectors General, the government officials charged with the inspection of all gaols in Ireland. These reports are the main source of information on the Gaol up to the 1870s.

A satirical cartoon by George Cruickshank entitled "Newgate Prison discipline, 1818", depicting the ugliness of unregulated association among prisoners.

The main cause of overcrowding was the use of the Gaol as a transportation depot. Prisoners from the north-eastern counties of Ireland who had been sentenced to transportation were transferred to Kilmainham before being sent on to Cork, from where they were eventually transported to Australia. The Inspectors General persistently complained of this practice in their annual reports, insisting that a proper routine would be impossible for as long as the Gaol was used as a holding area for transportees.

There were other chronic problems as well. In his report for 1809, the Inspector noted that good order in the Gaol was not helped by the fact that no distinction was made between the criminal and the insane. Lunatics were treated as criminals and imprisoned for the acts arising from their illness. (The practice of separating sane from criminally insane prisoners was not adopted until the 1870s.)

In 1817 an accidental fire caused extensive damage to the west wing. However it allowed for rebuilding on a much improved plan. Day rooms for male and female prisoners, where they could be given tasks to occupy them, were added.

The 1825 report considered the state of the Gaol to be well below that of other county prisons. The arrangements for the separation of male and female prisoners continued to be inadequate. There was insufficient accommodation at Kilmainham, with most prisoners having to share cells. The 1830 report named the county gaols of Dublin, Kilkenny, Tipperary and Fermanagh as the most deficient in the country.

The reports became increasingly critical during the 1830s as recommendations for improvements continued to be ignored. More cells were urgently required as there were now up to three or four prisoners in cells meant for one.

A decisive effort at improvement was at last made in 1840. The Grand Jury made a sum of £1,550 available to supply an additional 30 female cells. The Lord Lieutenant directed that Smithfield prison should be fitted out as a convict depot, easing finally the pressure of overcrowding at Kilmainham.

Plan of the Gaol in the 1840s showing recent improvements. The most significant is the addition of the extra block of women's cells (highlighted) to ease overcrowding in the women's section.

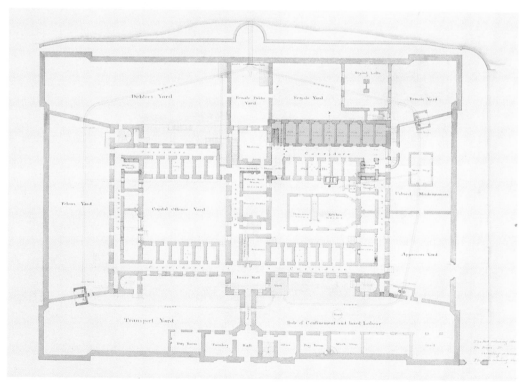

No sooner had these improvements been made however than Kilmainham was overwhelmed by the impact of the Great Famine. The mass of the people depended for their survival on a single crop, the potato. When the crop failed through blight, millions of them were threatened with starvation. The impact of the famine on Kilmainham first appears in the Inspector General's report for 1846 where he recommends 'a change in the dietary on account of the disease in the potato crop.' Only three years earlier the prison diet had been changed from meal to potatoes because potatoes were cheaper. Now, with potato blight rampant throughout the country, there was no choice but to introduce bread as a substitute.

Hunger knows no law. Hordes of desperate people sought relief wherever they could find it. The Gaol registers for the period show a dramatic increase in the number of food-related offences. A typical page for 1848 has the following entries: a man imprisoned for having three geese he could not account for; two young men jailed for attacking a bread cart; another for having 'bread and butter in his possession which had been stolen.' Under conditions of mass starvation a prison diet became a luxury. 'Larcenies have multiplied,' declared the Inspector in his 1848 report, 'because men will steal food rather than die.' To discourage people from deliberately offending, the prison diet was reduced to the minimum. But these measures did not stop the number of gaol deaths from climbing dramatically. In 1845 one person died in Kilmainham Gaol; the following year there were three; in 1847 twenty nine.

Sketch from the Illustrated London News *attempting to convey something of the suffering of the Great Famine.*

A page from the Gaol register for 1847. Note the food-related offences.

The problems for those running the prisons were made infinitely worse when the government, with spectacularly bad timing, introduced a Vagrant Act. Its effect was to compel magistrates to imprison all people found begging. As a result a host of destitute, filthy and diseased humanity swamped the prisons. With barely concealed outrage, the Inspector described the consequences in his 1847 report:

Numbers of these wretched creatures are obliged to lie on straw in the passages and dayrooms of the prison without a possibility of washing or exchanging their own filthy rags for proper apparel... Upon the necessity of passing this Act, it is not our place to pass an opinion, but of its effect upon the condition of the gaols we are painfully conscious. The committing of vagrants led to the introduction of fever and dysentery into a crowded prison and the sacrifice of many lives.

In 1849 there was a fourfold increase in the number of committals. Prisoners were five to a cell. Committals reached an all-time high in 1850 at 9,034 for the year. Dietary for able-bodied men consisted of seven ounces of meal and a pint of milk for breakfast, and a pound of bread and a pint of milk for dinner. Potatoes were only restored to the diet in 1855.

"Distress in the West of Ireland", A mother tends to her starving child, Illustrated London News

The year 1850, which more or less marked the end of the Great Famine, was a watershed year in the prisons, as it was in practically every aspect of Irish life. Up to a million people had died in the Famine and over a million had emigrated. A steep decline in the national population was matched by a dramatic decline in the prison population. With the famine crisis rapidly abating and with the completion of Mountjoy prison in 1850, the prison authorities looked forward to bringing about widespread reforms in the prison system generally.

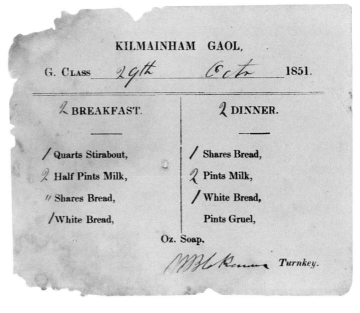

A Kilmainham Gaol ration voucher for 29 October, 1851. Though the allowances appear extremely meagre to modern eyes, they do reflect a vast improvement on the prison diet of only a few years previously at the height of the Famine. Note however that potatoes have not yet been returned to the diet.

"Distress in the West of Ireland", Sketch on famine conditions, Illustrated London News

Victorian Optimism:
The new East Wing (1861)

At Kilmainham the poor conditions in which women prisoners were kept provided the spur for the next stage of development. Remarkably, for an age that prided itself on a protective attitude towards the 'weaker sex', the conditions for women prisoners were persistently worse than for men. As early as his 1809 report the Inspector had observed that male prisoners were supplied with iron bedsteads while females 'lay on straw on the flags in the cells and common halls.' Half a century later there was little improvement. The women's section, located in the west wing, remained overcrowded. In his reports for the early 1850s, the Inspector persistently criticised the failure to provide separate cell accommodation for

There are no illustrations of the conditions for women prisoners in Irish jails during the nineteenth century. However this .sketch of "Female convicts at work during the silent hour, Brixton Prison" from The Criminal Prisons of London *by Henry Mayhew, (1861) gives some idea of the similar regime that would have applied in Irish jails. Note the similarity in design of the stairways and landings with those in Kilmainham's East Wing.*

women. He considered the solitude and silence of separate confinement to be particularly effective with women as it 'broke them into submission and sometimes softened them into repentance.'

It was this concern which apparently lay behind the decision taken in 1856 to build a new extension to the Gaol. It was not the women, however, who were to benefit from the bright and airy new wing. The men were to be transferred there, making room for the women in the older and gloomier west wing.

The Victorian age was the great age of prison design and construction. The Victorians had real faith in the power of prisons to reform offenders, and regarded prison architecture and design as a critical part of the process. In no age before or since have so many new prisons been built. As late as the 1970s, over forty percent of prisons in use in Great Britain and Ireland had been built during Victoria's reign.

The new Kilmainham extension, designed by John McCurdy, (one of whose recent commissions had been refurbishing Dublin's luxurious Shelbourne Hotel) displays two of the classic features of Victorian prison design. Firstly, an emphasis on the principle of observation: the doors of all cells on three floors face onto a single vaulted space, and each door has a spyhole. Prisoners, whether exercising together or alone in their cells, were in a position to be constantly observed. Secondly, a faith in the spiritually reforming powers of light: each cell window was set just below the ceiling, directing the prisoner's gaze upwards towards a patch of sky. The spectacular glass canopy over the main concourse allows the space to be flooded with light. When visiting the gaol as a young boy in the 1890s the dramatist Sean O'Casey (1880-1964) caught the mood and intention of the design. Recalling

Opposite:
Prison officers on the East Wing landing soon after it opened. At this stage the landings had only waist-high railings. All the landings were fully railed in towards the end of the century, presumably to prevent prisoners causing harm to themselves or their custodians. Note the carpeting on the ground floor, so that footfalls on the stone flags would not alert a prisoner as the warder approached his cell to observe him through the spyhole.

the experience later, he was reminded of some lines from a poem of Cardinal Newman's:

Lead, kindly light, amid the encircling gloom,
Lead Thou me on!
The night is dark, and I am far from home -
Lead Thou me on!
Keep Thou my feet; I do not ask to see
The distant scene, - one step enough for me.

It was hardly surprising then that the same Victorians considered deprivation of light to be one of the principal forms of punishment. The basement of the new building contained four punishment cells. Here a prisoner could face up to fourteen days solitary confinement on bread and water. The only light came through a small vent high up in the wall - and even this small chink could be reduced or eliminated by means of a slide on the outside.

East wing cell, 1890s.

The new extension was completed in 1861/62, and improvements to the female wing two years later.

The year 1877 saw major changes in prison administration in Ireland. Responsibility for running prisons passed from the County Grand Juries to a centralised General Prisons Board. The role of Inspector General was abolished. Under the new regime, male prisoners serving over a year and female prisoners serving over six months were transferred to Mountjoy Prison where surplus accommodation was available. The reformatory power of hard labour was considered most effective when packed

Meals being served to prisoners in their cells. This photograph is from an English prison, but a similar regime would have been followed in Kilmainham. Under this system, meals could be served to 300 prisoners in less than ten minutes.

into the early months of a sentence. Now, with only short-term prisoners being committed to Kilmainham, it became effectively a hard labour prison. The main forms of hard labour were stone-breaking and working the crank pump (two hours a day) which the governor had installed in 1862.

When the Gaol was first built public hangings took place at the front of the Gaol. However, from the 1820s onward very few hangings, public or private, took place at Kilmainham. For the first time in many years a prisoner was hanged in the Gaol in 1865. It was in this context that the Inspector's report for that year recommended the building of a railing at the front of the Gaol to prevent people gathering 'in times of excitement.' But it was only in 1883, when five of the Invincibles were hanged in the Gaol, that the railings were finally erected.

The twentieth century: From convict prison to Military Detention Barracks

From the late 1880s into the early years of the new century Kilmainham operated as a routine penal institution, unperturbed by any great political upheavals in the world outside its walls. The Irish prison population continued to decline dramatically. The Prisons Board began to look at ways of saving money by closing some prisons. Kilmainham was one of them. After a thousand or so prisoners had been transferred to Mountjoy Prison in 1909, the Gaol closed in February 1910 and was handed over to the military for their use. With the outbreak of the First World War in August 1914 its proximity to the Royal Hospital, Headquarters of British Forces in Ireland, made it a convenient place for billeting the overflow of recruits.

Kilmainham was used as a military detention centre for only a few weeks after the 1916 Rising. Once those detained were released or sent into internment in England and Wales the Gaol fell into disuse again. But the practice of using it as a military prison had been established. It was pressed into service once again by the British Army in 1920-21 at the height of the War of Independence, and by the Free State Army during the Civil War of 1922-23. When the last Republican prisoner was removed in July 1924, the Gaol was abandoned.

First floor landing (west wing) 1890s. It was in cells along this landing that most of the 1916 leaders were held prior to their execution.

PATRIOT PRISON

Kilmainham and
the nationalist tradition

Of the five nationalist rebellions that took place during the Gaol's lifetime, only two (1798 and 1916) were significant in military terms. However their historical importance has less to do with their military achievements than their symbolic effect. Just before the 1916 Rising, Patrick Pearse (1879-1916), the most ideologically influential of latter-day nationalist writers, reviewed the nationalist tradition up to his own day. He reserved his highest praise for those of his predecessors who had advocated open rebellion and given inspiration through their own self-sacrificing efforts. The cumulative effect of his survey was to give forceful expression to the idea of a tradition of undying nationalist aspiration erupting from generation to generation in open rebellion.

In the decades following independence the history of Ireland was taught with such singular focus on these rebellions that the impression of an oppressed people in ceaseless revolt was easily given. This of course was misleading. For most of the time between 1798 and 1916 Ireland remained calm, with political energies concentrated on reform by constitutional means. Daniel O'Connell's efforts to achieve Catholic Emancipation and Repeal of the Act of Union from the 1820s to the 1840s, and the push for Home Rule between 1886 and 1912, were the major political movements of nineteenth-century Ireland. On the whole, the armed rebellions tended to follow disillusionment with the failure of constitutional efforts, exemplified by the fact that many of the rebels were themselves disillusioned constitutionalists.

Sunken hopes: cartoon from 1912 reviewing a tradition of failed efforts at Irish political independence, ending with the failure that year of the Third Home Rule Bill.

Since the outbreak of the troubles in Northern Ireland in the late 1960s, all aspects of modern Irish history have been subjected to radical reassessment. In particular, the physical force tradition, as summed up by Pearse, has been the subject of intense debate, both moral and historical. However, those who set out to restore Kilmainham in the early sixties shared an unequivocal belief in the nobility of that tradition, and saw the Gaol itself as an eloquent monument to the patriotism and self-sacrifice of all those who had been imprisoned or died there in the cause of Irish political independence, whether they had sought that goal through constitutional means or by armed force. What follows is an account of the individual events that make up that tradition and the specific ways in which they were reflected in Kilmainham.

Wall mural depicting Patrick Pearse, West Belfast, 1982

The 1798 Rebellion

Theobald Wolfe Tone

In the eighteenth century, Ireland had its own parliament under the Crown, but it represented the interests of a narrow elite. The Catholic majority, along with Protestant Dissenters, were excluded. Inspired by Thomas Paine's *The Rights of Man* and the French Revolution, an alliance of Protestant Dissenters with Catholic leaders set up the Society of United Irishmen in 1791. Initially moderate in its aims, the Society's frustration at the repeated failure of government to grant political reform and Catholic emancipation led to its increasing radicalisation. In 1795 it was reconstituted as a secret oath-bound organisation dedicated to achieving political independence for Ireland. Its most able apologist, Theobald Wolfe Tone (1763-1798), described the movement's goal as 'to substitute the common name of Irishman in the place of the denominations of Protestant, Catholic and Dissenter', and to break the connection with England, 'the never failing source of all our political evils.'

The rebellion that eventually took place in pursuit of these principles in the summer of 1798 failed largely because the planned seizure of key buildings in Dublin, and a subsequent *coup d'état*, never occurred. The main rebel force was defeated in Wexford in July, and a small French force that landed in Mayo in August surrendered a few weeks later in Longford.

Henry Joy McCracken (1767-1798) from Belfast was one of the founders of the United Irishmen. He has the distinction of being the first political prisoner of note whose name is to be found in the Kilmainham Gaol register. He was arrested on 11 October, 1796, within months of the Gaol's opening. After his release he led the United Irishmen of Antrim in the rebellion and was subsequently hanged on 17 July, 1798.

Thomas Addis Emmet (1764-1827) came from a prominent Dublin family and was a leading member of the United Irishmen. He was arrested in February 1798 and taken to Kilmainham, where he languished before being sent into exile in 1802. The brothers Henry (1753-1798) and John Sheares (1756-1798) from Cork had been in France at the height of the Revolution and returned to Ireland to become two of the most radical members of the United Irishmen. They were detained in Kilmainham before being publicly hanged on 14 July, 1798.

Thomas Addis Emmet

Emmet's Rebellion of 1803

Robert Emmet (1778-1803) was the younger brother of Thomas Addis Emmet. While a student at Trinity College in 1798, he was expelled because of his outspoken sympathy for the United Irishmen. He went to France where he met Napoleon, who assured him that he was intending to invade England soon. Emmet returned home and began making preparations for a rebellion to coincide with the Anglo-French war. The war between France and England duly broke out early in 1803 and Emmet's plans intensified. But a premature explosion at a bomb factory forced him into a rising on 23 July, 1803. It was quelled within hours.

C: PAT MURPHY

Emmet was arrested on 25 August and taken to Kilmainham along with his housekeeper, Anne Devlin (1781-1851). Despite intense physical and psychological pressure, she refused to betray Emmet. She was held at the Gaol in wretched conditions for over two years and released in broken health. Because of her sufferings, she was the first woman to figure prominently in the list of nationalist heroes.

When Emmet was tried for High Treason on 19 September, he made a speech from the dock in which he laid down the following haunting challenge to future generations of nationalists: 'When my country takes her place among the nations of the earth, then, and not till then, let my epitaph be written.' He was taken from Kilmainham and executed at Thomas Street the following day.

Brid Brennan as Anne Devlin from Pat Murphy's film "Anne Devlin", shot partly on location in Kilmainham Gaol.

If the FRENCH land in Ireland, Oh, my Countrymen! meet them on the Shore with a Torch in one hand — a Sword in the other — receive them with all the destruction of War. Immolate them in their Boats before our Native Soil should be polluted by a Foreign Foe.

Contemporary cartoon of Robert Emmet making his speech from the dock.

Opposite: Late nineteenth century depiction of the Emmet execution scene at Thomas Street. (Inset: Emmet's death mask, Kilmainham Gaol collection)

Thomas Russell

Thomas Russell (1767-1803), a founding member of the United Irishmen, had been among the first political prisoners in Kilmainham in 1796. He tried to rescue Emmet but failed. He was taken to Downpatrick, Co. Down, where he was tried for High Treason and hanged outside the gaol gates.

Michael Dwyer (1771-1815) was the leader of a group of United Irishmen from County Wicklow. He was due to join Emmet's rebellion but never received a signal. He surrendered soon after and was lodged in Kilmainham. In 1805 Dwyer and his family were transported to Australia, where he pursued a career as a publican, sheep farmer, and police constable!

The Young Ireland Rebellion of 1848

The Young Ireland movement developed out of Daniel O'Connell's movement for Repeal of the Act of Union. As its name implies, it represented a younger generation who had grown impatient with O'Connell's moderate constitutionalism and what they saw as his end-

Formal portrait of William Smith O'Brien, signed by him while a prisoner in Kilmainham on August 31, 1848.

less tactical manoeuvring. John Mitchel (1815-75), one of the leading contributors to the movement's newspaper, *The Nation*, indicated that Young Ireland might ultimately consider using physical force. In 1846 they finally broke with the Repeal movement when O'Connell demanded that they disavow the use of force.

Consisting mostly of middle-class writers and intellectuals, the movement was never seriously placed to plan a successful rebellion. When revolution broke out in France in February 1848 it spurred one Young Irelander, William Smith O'Brien (1803-1864), to stage a protest rebellion he hoped would inspire a wider uprising. But what transpired was little more than a badly organised skirmish at Ballingarry, Co. Tipperary.

He and another Young Ireland leader, Thomas Francis Meagher (1822-67), were taken to Kilmainham. While awaiting trial, Smith O'Brien's son was baptised in the Gaol's Protestant chapel. Both men were sentenced to death, but this was commuted to transportation for life to Australia. O'Brien was released in 1854 and returned to Ireland in 1856, after which he played no further part in politics. Meagher escaped from Australia and made his way to America. On the outbreak of the Civil War he became Brigadier General of the New York Irish Brigade. After the war he entered politics to become Territorial Secretary and Acting Governor of Montana. But soon after he met an untimely death in a drowning accident.

John Mitchel was also transported to Australia. Though he had not been held in Kilmainham, he later wrote an account of his prison experiences and political beliefs entitled *Jail Journal*. It proved to be highly influential with subsequent generations of Irish nationalists, and established the published account of gaol experiences as a potent genre within the nationalist tradition.

The Fenian Rebellion of 1867

Some of those who had fled Ireland in the wake of the Young Ireland debacle went on to found the organisations that lay behind the next rebellion some twenty years later. John O'Mahony (1815-77) fled first to France and then onwards to the US. There in 1858 he founded an organisation called the Fenians and in the same year provided the money for James Stephens (1824 -1901) to found

Smith O'Brien (seated) and Meagher (standing, centre left) under guard in Kilmainham Gaol.

James Stephens

its Irish counterpart, the Irish Republican Brotherhood (IRB). Although the Irish and
American movements were separate, they became known collectively as the Fenians. The aim
of the new organisations, which were secret and oath-bound, was to overthrow British rule in
Ireland and establish a republic.

The main hope of external support for a rising in Ireland had shifted from France to
America. When the American Civil War broke out in 1861 large numbers of Irish Americans
joined Irish regiments on both sides. With the ending of the war in 1865, the American
Fenians became impatient for a rising, hoping to persuade officers and men recruited from
the Irish-American regiments to lead it. James Stephens' reluctance to stage a rising without
adequate preparation led to his overthrow as leader of the IRB in 1866. A network of
informers was meanwhile providing the government with detailed information on the rebels'
plans. Stephens was among those arrested in the swoops that followed. The rising, which
eventually went ahead in atrocious weather in March 1867, was soon defeated.

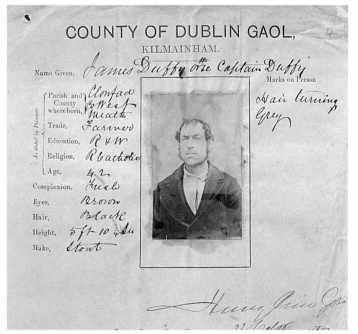

The rising's failure was followed by
the mass arrest of Fenian suspects. James
Stephens' daring escape from Dublin's
Richmond Prison in December 1865 had
shocked the authorities into a major
investigation of gaol security. As a result,
Kilmainham was designated the main place
of detention for Fenian suspects. Ordinary
convicts were moved to other gaols and
structural alterations were carried out to
turn it into a high-security prison. The
Inspector General's report of 1866
describes it as 'the most secure county
prison in the Kingdom.' This was a
significant moment in the history of the
Gaol and British penal history generally: it
was the first time that a place of detention had
been deliberately and exclusively adapted for
the reception of political prisoners.

Parnell and the 'Kilmainham Treaty'

The Great Famine did not see an end to suffering and hardship for those who struggled to make a living off the land. The spectre of famine loomed once again in the late 1870s when an economic slump, combined with failure of the corn crop in successive bad summers, led to a crisis. Dependent on the earnings from their crops, many farming tenants could no longer afford to pay their rents and were threatened with eviction by their landlords.

To help the tenant farmers protect themselves from exploitation and fight for better conditions, Michael Davitt (1846-1906) set up the Land League in Mayo in 1879. He was soon joined by the young leader of the Irish Parliamentary Party, Charles Stewart Parnell (1846-1891), who helped turn the tenants' campaign into a nation-wide agitation. As led by Parnell and Davitt, the Land League became a mass movement of popular disobedience exerting massive pressure on the government.

Michael Davitt

Charles Stewart Parnell around the time of his arrest. Soon after his release he grew a full beard, which he retained for the rest of his life.

Evicition scene, 1880s,
LAWRENCE COLLECTION, NATIONAL LIBRARY OF IRELAND

The campaign pressurised Gladstone's government into introducing a Land Act in 1881. Parnell's rejection of the Act and his continued defiance of the government led to his arrest on 13 October, 1881. A good many of his fellow MPs were arrested over the following days and lodged along with him in Kilmainham. There followed six months of negotiations between the British Prime Minister at Number 10 Downing Street and the Irish leader in Kilmainham Gaol. The conclusion of these negotiations, the so-called 'Kilmainham Treaty', was a major landmark in Irish constitutional history. Under its terms, Parnell undertook to cooperate with Gladstone and the Liberal Party in working towards a joint policy on Ireland. It is not too much of an exaggeration to say, therefore, that the course of the succeeding thirty two years of Irish constitutional history was set in Kilmainham Gaol in 1882. Parnell devoted the rest of his life until his untimely death in 1891 to the parliamentary campaign for Home Rule. After his death his successor, John Redmond (1856-1918), carried on with the campaign until it foundered on the outbreak of war in 1914.

MPs and other leading Parnellites soon followed their leader into Kilmainham. As is clear from this illustration and that of Parnell's cell (above) the prison regime was a good deal more relaxed for these distinguished inmates than for common prisoners. The Government feared that any grounds for rumours of ill-treatment would have worsened the already serious state of unrest in the country.

The Invincibles

The imprisonment of Parnell and other MPs had left the country without effective leadership. There was a dramatic increase in the general level of violence throughout the country. Secret oath-bound organisations were behind much of it. But Parnell's release from Kilmainham on 2 May 1882 was followed four days later by the most sensational event of all. On the morning of 6 May the new Chief Secretary for Ireland, Lord Frederick Cavendish, and his Under Secretary, Thomas Burke, were assassinated as they walked in the Phoenix Park. The assassinations were carried out by an offshoot of the Fenian movement calling themselves the Invincibles. One of their number, James Carey, turned informer. His revelations led to the execution in Kilmainham of five of the Invincibles between 14 May and 9 June 1883.

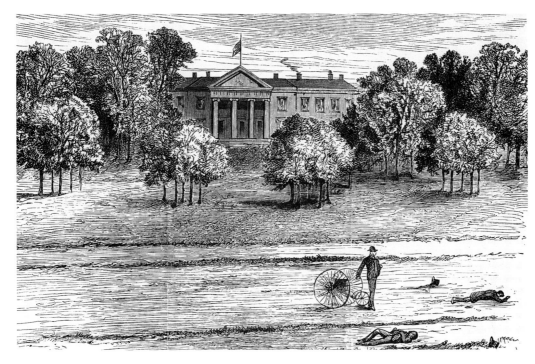

The murder scene in the Phoenix Park, directly opposite the Viceregal Lodge (now Áras an Uachtaráin, the Presidential residence) Illustrated London News, 1883.

"The Phoenix Park Murder Trials: The Prisoners brought to Kilmainham", Illustrated London News, 1883

The 1916 Rising

The origins of the 1916 Rising are complex, but one of its main sources lay in the extraordinary flowering of cultural nationalism that came to a head in the first decade of the century. The founding in 1893 of the Gaelic League, a movement to revive the Irish language, and the growth of a literary movement led by the dominant figure of W.B. Yeats (1865-1939), gave the younger generation a strong sense of a distinctively Irish cultural identity. Among the signatories to the 1916 Proclamation of the Irish Republic were three Irish-speaking poets, Patrick Pearse, Joseph Plunkett and Thomas MacDonagh.

The failure of the British government to implement the Third Home Rule Bill in 1912 disillusioned many young cultural nationalists, whose thoughts now began to turn towards

Sir Edward Carson, the Ulster Unionist Leader, at an Ulster Volunteer Rally (1912)

C: PUBLIC RECORD OFFICE, NORTHERN IRELAND

the possibility of wresting independence by means of physical force. In 1912 Ulster Unionists set up an armed Ulster Volunteer Force to resist Home Rule. It prompted the founding in Dublin in November 1913 of an Irish Volunteer Force to defend the claim to Home Rule.

At the outbreak of War in August 1914 the Volunteer movement split. The majority (about 200,000) followed the advice of the Parliamentary Party leader John Redmond and joined the war to fight for 'the freedom of small nations.' The remainder (about 10,000) followed Eoin MacNeill, the movement's founder, in his insistence that the Volunteers remain a national defence force only.

One of the Mauser rifles, landed from the Asgard.
(KILMAINHAM GAOL COLLECTION)

Mrs. Molly Childers (left) and Mary Spring Rice aboard the Asgard, handing ashore guns destined for the Irish Volunteers in July 1914. Many of the Mauser rifles ended up being used in the 1916 Rising.

"YOUR FIRST DUTY IS TO TAKE YOUR PART IN ENDING THE WAR"

Mr J.E. REDMOND. M.P.
at Waterford 23rd August 1915.

JOIN AN IRISH REGIMENT TO-DAY

Recruiting poster, 1914. John Redmond urged Irishmen to join the Great War against Germany.

Opposite. The General Post Office, headquarters of the Rising, photographed from the top of nearby Nelson's Pillar soon after the Rising ended.

James Connolly

The plot for a rising, taking advantage of Britain's distraction in the War, now began to take shape within the reduced Volunteer force. The veteran Fenian Thomas Clarke (1856-1916), a leading member of the IRB, was the nucleus around which younger men gathered and began planning a Rising. Meanwhile James Connolly (1868-1916), a socialist and trade union leader, had helped to set up a Citizen Army to defend the Dublin working class, who had been harshly dealt with by employers in an all-out strike in 1913. Connolly had come to the conclusion that socialism could only follow from political independence on a national basis. He joined forces with the IRB group in the weeks just before the Rising.

Original copy of the 1916 Proclamation sent by Thomas Clarke, the first of the signatories, to his wife Kathleen on Easter Monday 1916.

POBLACHT NA H EIREANN.
THE PROVISIONAL GOVERNMENT
OF THE
IRISH REPUBLIC
TO THE PEOPLE OF IRELAND.

IRISHMEN AND IRISHWOMEN : In the name of God and of the dead generations from which she receives her old tradition of nationhood, Ireland, through us, summons her children to her flag and strikes for her freedom.

Having organised and trained her manhood through her secret revolutionary organisation, the Irish Republican Brotherhood, and through her open military organisations, the Irish Volunteers and the Irish Citizen Army, having patiently perfected her discipline, having resolutely waited for the right moment to reveal itself, she now seizes that moment, and, supported by her exiled children in America and by gallant allies in Europe, but relying in the first on her own strength, she strikes in full confidence of victory.

We declare the right of the people of Ireland to the ownership of Ireland, and to the unfettered control of Irish destinies, to be sovereign and indefeasible. The long usurpation of that right by a foreign people and government has not extinguished the right, nor can it ever be extinguished except by the destruction of the Irish people. In every generation the Irish people have asserted their right to national freedom and sovereignty : six times during the past three hundred years they have asserted it in arms. Standing on that fundamental right and again asserting it in arms in the face of the world, we hereby proclaim the Irish Republic as a Sovereign Independent State, and we pledge our lives and the lives of our comrades-in-arms to the cause of its freedom, of its welfare, and of its exaltation among the nations.

The Irish Republic is entitled to, and hereby claims, the allegiance of every Irishman and Irishwoman. The Republic guarantees religious and civil liberty, equal rights and equal opportunities to all its citizens, and declares its resolve to pursue the happiness and prosperity of the whole nation and of all its parts, cherishing all the children of the nation equally, and oblivious of the differences carefully fostered by an alien government, which have divided a minority from the majority in the past.

Until our arms have brought the opportune moment for the establishment of a permanent National Government, representative of the whole people of Ireland and elected by the suffrages of all her men and women, the Provisional Government, hereby constituted, will administer the civil and military affairs of the Republic in trust for the people.

We place the cause of the Irish Republic under the protection of the Most High God, Whose blessing we invoke upon our arms, and we pray that no one who serves that cause will dishonour it by cowardice, inhumanity, or rapine. In this supreme hour the Irish nation must, by its valour and discipline and by the readiness of its children to sacrifice themselves for the common good, prove itself worthy of the august destiny to which it is called.

Signed on Behalf of the Provisional Government,
THOMAS J. CLARKE.
SEAN Mac DIARMADA.   THOMAS MacDONAGH.
P. H. PEARSE.   EAMONN CEANNT.
JAMES CONNOLLY.   JOSEPH PLUNKETT.

The Rising began with Pearse's reading of the Proclamation of a Republic from the steps of the GPO on Easter Monday morning, 24 April, 1916. The rebels held out for a week at strategic buildings around Dublin. But eventually, recognising the hopelessness of the situation with British forces massing against them, and increasingly concerned at the level of civilian casualties, they surrendered on Saturday 29 April.

Opposite:
Front page of the Daily Mirror for May 8, 1916. It focuses on the tragic circumstances of MacDonagh and Plunkett's executions. They left behind two widowed sisters, Muriel and Grace Gifford. The Countess Markievicz is unjustly portrayed here as the evil influence behind their deaths.

TRAGIC ROMANCE OF COUNT PLUNKETT AND HIS SONS

The Daily Mirror

CERTIFIED CIRCULATION LARGER THAN THAT OF ANY OTHER DAILY PICTURE PAPER

No. 3,912. Registered at the G.P.O as a Newspaper. MONDAY, MAY 8, 1916. One Halfpenny.

COUNTESS WHO WRECKED TWO YOUNG LIVES : HOW SHE LURED THE REBELS TO THEIR FOLLY.

Count Plunkett.

Joseph Plunkett.

Thomas MacDonagh.

Countess Markievicz (x) and her sister Eva at Lissadell, their home in Sligo. It is a recent snapshot.

The sordid Dublin rebellion has produced one romance, a pathetic story of young lives ruined by another. A few hours before he faced the firing party which carried out the death sentence Joseph Plunkett, who is said to be a son of Count Plunkett, the holder of a Papal title, was married in his cell to Miss Grace Gifford, a daughter of a Dublin solicitor and a lady of considerable artistic attainments. Her sister Muriel was the wife of Thomas Macdonagh, another leader who has been shot. Thus the two sisters were widowed within twenty-four hours of each other. And behind all this tragedy looms the figure of the Countess Markievicz, the daughter of Sir Henry Gore-Booth, Bart. "It was she," says Mrs. Gifford, "who dragged the two men into it." Count Plunkett and the Countess were both sentenced to death, but both sentences have been commuted

In 1911 Kilmainham Gaol had ceased functioning as a convict prison and had been taken over by the Army as a detention barracks for military prisoners. As military prisoners, the insurgents were now divided between Richmond Barracks and the Gaol. All of the leaders (except the wounded Connolly) were detained at Richmond Barracks, where they were court-martialled and sentenced to death. They were taken to Kilmainham Gaol on the eve of their executions, where they spent their last hours and wrote their last letters.

Among the individual tragedies now unfolding in the Gaol, one extraordinarily poignant case stands out. On the evening of 3 May, hours before his execution, Joseph Plunkett, already desperately ill with tuberculosis, married the young artist Grace Gifford in the Gaol's Catholic chapel. A few hours later, he faced the firing squad in the stone-breaker's yard, one of fourteen to be executed there between 3 and 12 May.

Eamon de Valera
under arrest in
Richmond Barracks
following his
surrender. Though
sentenced to death, this
was commuted to life
imprisonment because
of his American
citizenship.

De Valera's Volunteer tunic.

KILMAINHAM GAOL COLLECTION

The War of Independence and
Civil War, 1919-24

Previous rebellions had followed the pattern of fires that, after briefly flaring, were quenched to a few sparks - sparks that would smoulder for a generation or so before flaring once again in open rebellion. General Maxwell, the man charged with the job of quenching the 1916 rebellion, was determined that this time even the sparks would be utterly extinguished. However, his means, execution and internment, were to prove explosive.

As the rebels were marched along the quays after the rebellion they were jeered at by angry crowds. This anger at the destruction of the city probably reflected the broad popular mood. But the executions changed everything. Their apparent vindictiveness swung the popular mood to one of resentment and outrage. This was compounded by the imposition of martial law and aggravated in the following years by the attempt to impose conscription. The poetry and prose of Pearse, Connolly, MacDonagh and Plunkett began to appear in popular editions. They told a story of heroic and patriotic intentions. Gradually, many people came to see them no longer as reckless adventurists, but as men who had sacrificed themselves clear-sightedly to the cause of an independent Ireland.

Two prisoners under escort approaching Kilmainham Gaol, with the boundary wall of the Royal Hospital in the background.

FRAMED: (L) Roger Casement - executed London (R) Thomas Kent - executed Cork.
BACK ROW LEFT TO RIGHT: - Willie Pearse, Thomas MacDonagh, Sean Heuston, Michael Mallin, Sean MacDermott, Michael O'Hanrahan, Edward Daly, Con Colbert.
FRONT ROW LEFT TO RIGHT: (signatures) Patrick Pearse, Major John McBride, Thomas Clarke, Eamon Ceannt, James Connolly, Joseph Plunkett

Above left: 1916 commemorative medal, depicting the Dying Cúchulainn, after Oliver Sheppard's sculpture in the GPO.
Above right: Commemorative poster of the 1916 leaders (late 1916). It was not long after the Rising before a range of such material began appearing, helping to mould the popular mood in its favour.

Hundreds of those who had fought in 1916 were interned in camps in England and Wales. During their captivity, young men like Michael Collins (1891-1922) developed a single-minded and professional determination to achieve the Republic announced in the 1916 Proclamation.

The Sinn Féin victory in the general election of December 1918 was followed by the setting up of the first Dáil, or Irish parliament, in January 1919. One of the first acts of the new Dáil was to make a Declaration of Independence based on the 1916 Proclamation. This defiant act led rapidly to full confrontation. British forces in Ireland were soon engaged in an all-out guerrilla war with the Dáil's military wing, the Irish Republican Army (IRA). When the British government introduced two special units, the Auxiliaries and the Black and Tans, to help contain the situation, their brutal and undisciplined behaviour only served to strengthen popular sympathy for the Republicans.

DAIL EIREANN, AN CHEAD TIONOL, 21 EANAIR, 1919.

Sreath 1.—(i dtosach)—S. O'Dochartaigh, S. O. hAodha, S. O'Ceallaigh, Conte Pluingcéad, C. Brugha, S. T. O'Ceallaigh, P. O'Maille, S. Breathnach, T. O'Ceallaigh.   Sreath 2.—S. MacSuibhne, C. O. hUigin, D. O'Buachala, E. O'Dubhgain, P. Béaslaoi, An Dr. O'Riain, An Dr. O'Cruadhlaoigh, P. Mac an Bhaird, P. O'Maoldomhnaigh, R. Suataman.   Sreath 3— R. Bartuin, R. O'Maolchatha, C. O'Coileain, P. O'Seanachain, S. de Burca.

At the height of 'The Troubles' (as the conflict came to be known), the empty Kilmainham was once more pressed into service. In 1920, as the War of Independence intensified, it was opened up to receive the swelling numbers of Republican prisoners. Makeshift watch towers were placed on top of each of the Gaol's four perimeter walls. The soldiers manning them had orders to shoot escapees on sight. But despite these security measures three prisoners, Ernie O'Malley, Simon Donnelly and Frank Teeling, managed to escape on the evening of 14 February, 1921 with the aid of a sympathetic Welsh soldier.

War of Independence: Republican prisoners attending Mass in the Gaol's East wing. This photograph was taken by one of the prisoners using a box camera, indicating that the political prisoners were afforded privileges not accorded common convicts.

In June 1921 the six county state of Northern Ireland came into being. The following month a Truce was declared to allow for negotiations between the Republicans and the British government. The Gaol emptied once again. There followed extensive and intricate negotiations, resulting in the Treaty of December 1921. However when the Treaty, which stopped far short of recognising the Republic declared in 1919, was debated in the Dáil, it proved deeply divisive. Though the Treaty was passed by a narrow majority in favour of accepting a twenty-six county Free State with limited independence under the Crown, tensions between pro- and anti-Treaty factions grew over the following months and erupted in Civil War in June 1922.

The new Free State government now used the Gaol as one of a number of places of detention for their Republican opponents in the Civil War. Michael Collins, Chief of Staff of the Free State Army, asked his friend Sean Ó Muirthuile to take charge of the prison. After much agonising he accepted, 'lest it might be considered that I was shirking a difficult duty.' It was indeed a difficult duty. Many of the prisoners he was now guarding were former comrades from the War of Independence.

War of Independence: Auxiliaries, one of the special units drafted in to deal with the crisis, searching civilians along the Quays in Dublin, 1920.

Mollie Gill was one of the Cumann na mBan prisoners in Kilmainham in 1923.

At first the Gaol was used solely for male prisoners, but over 150 untried Republican women prisoners were transferred there in April 1923. Among them was Maud Gonne McBride (1866-1953), famously beloved of W.B. Yeats, and formerly the wife of John McBride (1865-1916), who was one of the fourteen executed in the Gaol in 1916. But she was not the only woman in this extraordinary situation. Nora Connolly, daughter of James Connolly, and Grace Plunkett, wife of Joseph Plunkett, were also among the women prisoners. In a letter to her mother in April 1923 Nora Connolly wrote, with an understatement no doubt designed to spare her mother's feelings, 'it is a bit depressing and a bit of a strain to spend Easter in the jail where Papa was executed.' Another prisoner, Dorothy Macardle, wrote with less restraint:

The sense of accumulated tragedy, endless sacrifice, the never ceasing persecution of those who stand for Ireland's freedom, has been terribly oppressive in this gloomy and evil reputed jail. The very stones of our exercise yard speak to us always of the blood that stained them in that awful week of May 1916.

It eased the trauma somewhat when the governor allowed them to hold a small ceremony at Easter in the yard where their dear ones had been executed.

Civil War: A group of Free State officers outside the Gaol; during the War, Republican prisoners were guarded by Free State troops.

The women found conditions appalling. Ironically, the women's section was the same dark and dismal west wing that had been the subject of such persistent complaint in the previous century. But the men, despite having been given the brighter and comparatively more cheerful East Wing, found conditions just as bad. The years of disuse since 1910 had taken their toll on the fabric of the building. There was one toilet for 130 men and virtually every pane of glass in the building had been broken.

Grace Gifford

Civil War graffiti from one of the cells in the women's wing.

> A FEW MEN FAITHFUL AND A DEATHLESS DREAM."

On her arrest Maud Gonne went on hunger strike. Yeats was meanwhile a Senator of the new Free State. Following representations he made on her behalf she was released on 27 April 1923, twenty days after her arrest. By 30 April most of the women had been moved, though women prisoners continued to be held here until the end of September, 1923.

Following Michael Collins's death in an ambush in August 1922, the Civil War became increasingly bitter. The government introduced emergency legislation, making it a capital offence to be caught in possession of a weapon. It was under these regulations that the first four Republican prisoners executed in the Civil War were shot in Kilmainham in November 1922.

Exhausted Republican forces eventually conceded defeat in May 1923. By this stage the jails were crammed with Republican prisoners. Gradually, over the coming year, they were removed. Eamon de Valera, the last prisoner to be held in Kilmainham, was released on 16 July, 1924. The Gaol closed and was abandoned to the elements. The sense of 'accumulated tragedy', as Dorothy Macardle had put it, had grown too great. Henceforth, the Gaol's only captive would be its recent history of bitter memories.

Campaign medal, War of Independence, 1919-21.

Jack B. Yeats's painting Communicating with Prisoners *(1924), based on an incident at Kilmainham Gaol. Relatives used to shout messages to prisoners in the top floor cells of the East Wing from along the South Circular Road.*

Ruin and Restoration

In 1936, when the question of what to do with Kilmainham came up for government consideration, an editorial in the *Wicklow People* newspaper offered the view that the place should be 'pulled down and its site made a playground for children, after suitably marking and commemorating the graves of those executed there.' The wounds of Civil War were still fresh and healing slowly. Kilmainham was one of the places most strongly associated with that bewildering period. The government decided to do nothing, and allowed the building to continue its descent into ruin.

Time however wrought a change of feeling. For the veterans of the 1916-23 period, bitter personal memories were gradually subsumed into the idea of a nationalist tradition greater than their individual sufferings. And so the first impulse to restore Kilmainham was to come eventually from the very men and women who had hitherto found good reason to acquiesce in its ruin and obliteration.

The Catholic Chapel before restoration (compare with the restored Chapel, above p.34)

In 1960 a Board of Trustees, consisting largely of veterans of the 1916-23 period, was set up with the object of restoring the Gaol as a national monument. Over the following twenty years a force of voluntary workers laboured to restore it. Their first major goal was to bring the Gaol, which they had found in a state of advanced ruin, to a condition where it would make a fitting venue for celebrating the fiftieth anniversary of the 1916 Rising in 1966. In April of that year, the President of Ireland, Eamon de Valera, who had the distinction of being Kilmainham's last prisoner, was shown around the Gaol by the Trustees.

The voluntary workers went on to consolidate their achievement by roofing, securing and restoring the entire building - an epic feat of voluntary effort and enthusiasm achieved without the support of government grants. Instead, the Trustees proved themselves adept at generating revenue, most notably through film location fees. Many famous films including *The Quare Fellow* (1965), *The Italian Job* (1969), *The Last Remake of Beau Geste* (1977) and more recently *In the Name of the Father* (1993), have used Kilmainham as a location.

In 1986 the Board of Trustees handed the upkeep and running of Kilmainham Gaol into state care under the Office of Public Works. As part of the transfer agreement a Board of Visitors was set up. The Board offers its advice on developments at the Gaol and conducts annual and other commemorative events in honour of those patriots and patriotic events associated with Kilmainham.

Daniel Day-Lewis as Gerry Conlon in "In The Name of the Father", shot on location in Kilmainham Gaol, 1993.

KILMAINHAM GAOL	IRISH HISTORY	GENERAL HISTORY
1786: Construction of Gaol begins		
		1789: Outbreak of French Revolution, Fall of Bastille
1796: Gaol opens Henry Joy McCracken	Dec: Wolfe Tone arrives with French fleet in Bantry Bay	
1798: Thomas Addis Emmet Henry and John Sheares	United Irish Rebellion	
	1801: Act of Union between Great Britian and Ireland	
1803: Aug: Robert Emmet Anne Devlin December: Michael Dwyer	July: Emmet Rebellion	England declares war on France Napoleon declares himself Emperor
		1814: Battle of Waterloo
1817: Fire in West wing; part of Gaol rebuilt. Potatoes replace bread for Dinner	Foundation stone laid down for Wellington monument, Phoenix Park	Jane Austin dies
1826: Prisons Act: Official Visiting Board of Superintendents set up for Irish Prisons		Death of Thomas Jefferson, author of The American Constitution
	1829: Catholic Emancipation	
1832: Lack of potatoes results in temporary return to oats as main element in diet	Irish Reform Bill widens franchise and increases Irish representation at Westminister from 100-105 seats	Reform act widens electoral franchise
1840: 30 new cells added for female prisoners		
1845: Diet once again changed from potatoes to oats	Great Famine begins	
1848: William Smith O'Brien Thomas Francis Meagher	Young Ireland Rebellion Start of Dun Laoghaire - Hollyhead mail boat service	"The Year of Revolution": Rebellions in countries throughout Europe
	1849: Queen Victoria visits Ireland	
1850: Highest number of prisoners ever recorded in Kilmainham; overcrowding from Famine	Mountjoy Prison completed	The poet William Wordsworth dies
	1851: Census shows decline of 1$^{1/2}$ million in population since 1841 census	Great Exhibition, Crystal Palace, London
	1853: Ending of transportation to Australia	Dickens' Bleak House is published
		1855-56: Crimean War
1858: Work begins on new East wing	James Stephens founds Irish Republican Brotherhood	
		1860: Outbreak of American Civil War
1862: New East wing completed		
	1865: Nov: James Stephens escapes from Richmond prison	End of American Civil War
1866: Kilmainham turned into top-security prison to receive Fenian suspects		American Fenians attack Canada

KILMAINHAM GAOL	IRISH HISTORY	GENERAL HISTORY
	1867: March: Outbreak of Fenian Rebellion	Dec: Fenian explosion at Clerkenwell Prison, London
	1869: Friedrich Engels, communist writer, visits Ireland	Suez Canal opens
		1871: Franco-Prussian War
1877: Kilmainham turned into hard labour prison for short-term convicts; long-term convicts moved to Mountjoy prison	General Prisons Board established to supervise prison standards throughout Ireland; post of Inspector General abolished	Queen Victoria declared Empress of India
	1879: Michael Davitt founds the Land League	
1881: Nov: *C.S. Parnell* arrested and taken to Kilmainham	Aug: Gladstone's second Land Act	
1882: 3 May: Parnell and other MPs released	5 May: Invincibles assassinate Cavendish and Burke in Phoenix Park	
1883: Five of the Invincibles hanged in Kilmainham		Krakatoa, East of Java, erupts
	1893: Founding of the Gaelic league	Second Home Rule Bill fails
		1899-1902: Boer War
1910: Gaol closes, becomes Military Detention Centre	Edward Carson becomes leader of Irish Unionists	George V crowned; Mark Twain dies
	1913: Formation of Ulster Volunteers; Home Rule Bill passed	
		1914: Outbreak of World War 1
1916: May 3-12: Fourteen leaders of Rising executed in Gaol	April 23-30: Easter Rising James Joyce's *Portrait of the Artist as a Young Man* published	July: Battle of Somme
	1918: Sinn Féin wins landslide in General Election	End of World War 1
	1919: Meeting of first Dáil; Outbreak of War of Independence	Versailles Treaty signed; Alcock and Brown first to fly Atlantic
	1920: Government of Ireland Act leads to setting up of Northern Ireland	
1921: Gaol reopens to receive Republican prisoners	July: truce declared; negotiations follow December: Anglo-Irish Treaty signed in London	
1922: June: Gaol begins to fill up with Republican prisoners arrested in Civil War. November: Four Republican prisoners executed in Kilmainham	June: General Election - large majority for pro-Treaty Sinn Féin Aug: Michael Collins killed in ambush	James Joyce's *Ulysses* published in Paris
1923: April: Women Republican prisoners moved to Kilmainham, where they go on hunger-strike. Among them are *Grace Gifford*, wife of Joseph Plunkett, *Nora Connolly*, daughter of James Connolly, and *Maud Gonne*, former wife of John McBride	May: Civil War ends Aug: de Valera arrested Sept: Irish Free State enters League of Nations	
1924: July: Transfer of Eamon de Valera, last Republican prisoner; Gaol closes	Sean O'Casey's *Juno and the Paycock* opens at Abbey Theatre	Lenin, leader of the Russian revolution, dies.
1960: Restoration Society sets about restoring Kilmainham as a memorial		